The Academics Brains and Recreation Logics
The Bright Thoughts

By

Bernard Benson Sarfo

The Academics Brains and Recreation Logics

Bernard Benson Sarfo

Published by Bernard Benson Sarfo, 2024.

THE ACADEMICS BRAINS AND RECREATION LOGICS

First edition. April 5, 2024.

Copyright © 2024 Bernard Benson Sarfo.

ISBN: 979-8224397617

Written by Bernard Benson Sarfo.

Also by Bernard Benson Sarfo

The Fact Among Facts (1st)
The Fact Among Facts

Standalone
The Youth Murderer
Be Original Not a Copy
The Christians Science or Scholarship
Precious than Paradise
Habit makes future
A shelter from storm and rain
The Science of Life
The Strongest Lion Knockback
The Perfect and Inspiring City
Above Hope, Faith and Love
The Hero's Brave Decisions
The Weakest Among Plants
The Hero's Brave Decisions
Doing Above The Ability
The Wisdom Beyond Power And Greatness
Heavier Than the Heavens
The Academics Brains and Recreation Logics

Dedication

I dedicate this book to everyone in the world today.

'When wisdom entered into your heart, and knowledge is pleasant unto your soul, discretion shall preserve you, understanding shall keep you' (Proverbs 2:10, 11).

Introduction

There are many activities that consuming our time and cause us much trouble. But others do not consider the life and what it is about, then engaging themselves in the things that cannot feed the soul for eternity.

There are also things done on earth that make us suckers but we do not mind doing them. Others are also wasting their time on valueless things. Many people have become slaves due to the kind of the trade they engage themselves.

Life consist of the entire activities goes on every day but the issues of life set up our fate. Many have missed their role as human beings.

This book is to let us consider our activities on each day, then to make us know the facts of everyday life. To know the outcome of the activities we engage ourselves in.

We cannot live in the world without knowledge and cannot develop well without understanding the knowledge gain. We must consider the life well and manage to the exact point. Our nature as human beings has no likeness concerning the creatures in this world. God created the world out of nothing and the world cannot have its likeness or anything that can be compared.

The heavens and earth are the containers or the house for all creatures. Every creature has its kind or likeness or the same kind.

Here all nature has its kind and likeness in which it came from. The original being of any creature has its form and identity. That is, every living creature has it kind and likeness.

The world has its original creatures and the source in which it came from or the mothers of creation. The earth is the mother of all creatures and the original source of every living and non-living things.

Without the earth, there are no creatures and without God, there are no heavens and the earth or the world. So, this world has its original source and the creator.

There are no copies of the heavens and the earth in anywhere whatsoever except what we see and live in it today. Again there is no other God apart from the one who created the heavens and the earth.

What do I mean? There are no copies creatures but there are the young ones through the birth of those beings. God did not create the copies of beings or creatures but the original beings and their young ones through birth.

If there is a copy of this earth, then there will be a copy of human beings but not the original ones. If not, there are no copies of human beings and other creatures. What do I mean?

In fact, any act or conduct or doings which are contrary to the law of God are not the unique one. What do I want us to learn? Any human being is unique and has what makes him or her uniqueness.

There is no one who does not have what makes his or her uniqueness. My concern for this topic is to let you know that you have what makes you and your ability as a person. You can do what no one can do accept you and can make the difference without likeness.

Why not maintain your originality and do things on your own to prevent bondage life? You need to be active and prudent, do not depend on someone's command and act, but try to do what you can by your own effort and manage.

We all need to keep in mind that, everyone has what makes life better and can do what no one can do in terms of skills and thought.

Contents

20. What is your interest?

21. What are your daily events?

22. Sensible but destitute

1. Uphold your beauty

You have what makes you and you can do what no one can do. Why making yourself as nothing and thinking different from your ability?

Can you change your physical being or can you turn to an animal? Never disregard the little you have but keep it and make it profitable. Do you know you can make a difference no one has ever made before?

Is there something different about you? Yes, there is something unique about you? Maybe you did not know.

Do not disregard your inner being or throw the precious Jewells away from your house. Do not toss your confident away and never let someone snatch your gold. That is, keep what you have and cherish it.

You have what no one has and without yours, there will be a lost innovation and precious idea. Do not take things for granted and do not throw your beauty for money sake. Be prudent and maintain the least as well as the big.

Do not cover the truth for money sake and do not lie for profit. Why die before your time? Keep on doing well and never stop giving, keep on in good works and never be discouraged for doing good.

It is hard to maintain your beauty due to the world condition. But be determined and die for the truth.

Do not dress anyhow and do not eat abusively to disregard your maker. But be decent in all your doings.

Keep your time to fulfil your goal and keep on progressing for the sake of helping others. It is not good to be selfish but let others praise you on your good works and supports.

Share what you have but do not be dishearten of doing that. You have something in you which surpass than other ones. Try and multiply it for the sake of others.

Do not keep the best for your own benefit but let others benefit than you and then fulfil the greatest love and receive an abundant blessing. Try to be alert but be silent on frivolous talk to keep your beauty.

It is not good to laugh on serious matters but keeps your mouth shut to maintain your wisdom. Keep yourself from corrupting and then gain understanding; discernment and wisdom for your progress.

It is late to say you are sorry, once you close your eyes on good things to let bad things go on. You need to keep yourself for profit but not lost.

Consider your identity always and know how to step your foot. Do not destroy your originality and make things worse and abhorring. Why destroy your diamond and gold? Do not be proud but fear God and keeps your steps well.

Do not praise yourself when you do well. Do not be too pompous but be modest to maintain your uniqueness. Try to seek for the weak ones and help them. Be merciful as your Father who is in Heaven is merciful.

Do not throw your good taste for money but accept your condition in all matters of life. Keeps your light shining for the benefit of others who are in darkness? Do not support unnecessary talks but have time for yourself and others salvation.

Be not wise at your own estimation but be humble and do things right. It is not good to say you are sorry by pretending but it is good to say sorry from the correct heart.

What do I mean? Do not close your eyes and do things wrong and seek forgiveness but try to prevent damage before cure.

Do not be hard but be flexible and receive respect. Always know your right but consider others too. Be faithful and manageable to keep precious things for the future generation.

Do not destroy the set standard but maintain it. Means keep the laws and maintain a peaceful atmosphere. Be forceful and vigilant to promote uniqueness but not disunity. It is good to have fun but be watchful and then to prevent shamefulness.

Do not reveal your friend secretes to others for your own damage but build a wall on it to keep your friendship. There are bad times and a condition but there are good time and condition.

But do not be discouraged when you are hurt by a storm. Keep on managing and build your city. It is not best to say I am further up but it is best to say I am fine by God grace.

Life cannot be fair always, but it is permitted to do things wrong but make a profit through hardship conditions to better your lot.

It is not lawful to break and steal because you are poor, but you must keep the law. Do not threaten because of your richness.

Do not fornicate because of the heat of lust; it is a law-breaking. Do not be annoyed through provocation but take heart and know how to move and talk.

Do not go to the right or left without carefulness. You cannot do the single of all these things but allow God to do it for you and then maintain your beauty.

2. Be Faithful

The world has so many incidence and records concerning human behaviour. In life, there are lessons which prove the beauty of everything we do or perform.

Many people have failed due to their act and behaviour. And there is no light without darkness and the light cannot be necessary without darkness. Action speaks louder than words and the word cannot be proving without action.

Faithfulness makes the difference between light and darkness and it brings cheerfulness to the soul. It is not good to make yourself lukewarm but it is good to be warm or cold.

What do I mean? Let your yes be yes and your no is no. You need to be light than to be light and darkness at the same time.

Do not deceive yourself and others for you are going to carry what the whole world cannot carry. Faithfulness heals the soul and revives the spirit.

Do not mislead others by your false message and never be salt-less without real taste. Let others praise you for your good works and with your plain talk. Do not mix water and oil in your mouth.

Be straight forward with your words but do not twist words with lies to destroy trees in your garden. Means do not pollute those around you with your false speech.

Be faithful but not a liar make your word heal the soul and be at peace. In fact, faithfulness builds the city and makes progress in life. Your words are your magistrates and your actions are your witness. What you do and say today will prove your truthfulness in the future.

Do not deceive by your appearance and never pretend to be light whiles you know it is not factual. It is wickedness to pretend to be light whiles your doings are contrary.

This world rotates and there are stages in the movement. You cannot be the same as you are in today. So, never deceive and do not pretend, for you will one day account for it.

Be faithful and mind your word. Be original not a copy; let your word proof your personality and make difference by your truth. Many people have lost their dignity and their glory through their words.

Others have disgraced themselves by their lies. The world is going into destruction through lies of those who dwell on it, and the truth has tremble on the ground.

Do not force your words to be factual whiles know you are deceiving. Be faithful but not a liar; be gentle but not a pretender, be smart but not as a thief.

Maintain your faithfulness and do not lie for a favour but approve yourself for good use. Never put yourself into trouble through lies but consider your speech and make your words fruitful. Let your words be simple and meaningful to your audience.

Do not rush in your speech but be careful when delivering a message. It is not good to shout but it is good to blend in some time. But in all, do not lie when giving out your message.

It is better to make simple messages than to prolong your message. Why because it is possible to make a mistake and lie at the same time. Be aware and make things decent but do not disgrace yourself in the area you have not been there before.

Means do not discuss the lessons you do not understand. Else, you will lie and disgrace yourself through inconsistent speech. But always watch out and control yourself in position without wrong comments later on.

Faithfulness controls peace and makes things better and encouraging. Do not make news where there are no happenings. Do not pollute the air by your false message but make the air blow at ease.

Be faithful when you buy; be faithful when you exchange, be faithful when you walk and talk. You can build a city by faithfulness and you can destroy the city through unfaithfulness.

Faithfulness makes things whole and stability. If you want to progress in life and live longer then be faithful. Be faithful to your master; be faithful to your servant and everyone. You can damage the whole city through your false news.

Do not build your city with lies and build your walls with unfaithfulness. Else, the mountain will talk and destroy your city at the end. Means never deceive others and earn your belongings and then disgrace yourself at the end.

Try to make ways when you are delivering a speech and polish your words with good salt. That is, tell the truth and let your words be a benefit to the viewers. Always build on truth and have peace of mind.

Do not fear to tell the truth and consider nothing when you are on the right path. Your spiritual strength; your thinking ability, your continuous peace and your health completeness stand on your truth.

If you want to build Heaven on the earth, then start to build the truth in all matters of life. Do not let others force you to tell the truth but let it be your preferred food and eat every day.

Be faithful and do not be shy and tell the truth but be bold and consider nothing, to tell the truth. Let your words be simple and true, but do not deceive by your appearance.

Be hasty, to tell the truth, and never mind the outcome. Be faithful in all things and continue in faithfulness until you die in it.

3. Be Moderate

Gentleness surpasses name and beauty; it is wealth for a good name and the sister of understanding. Gentleness brings success and beauty and it is a key that open doors for progress.

It is not better to have a good name without gentleness or kind. Beautiful life and understanding stand on gentleness.

One thing we need to know is that without gentleness the people cannot progress and do things well. To be gentle is to be temperate and to be temperate is to be sensible.

The world development and peace stand on kindness. The beauty of this world portrait in gentleness and the beauty of nature show its gentility.

Gentle consist of carefulness; integrity and moderation. In fact, in order to be great in life and prosper depends on kindness.

Many people disregard gentleness and live as they wish. And others want money than gentility or kindness life. But one thing we need to know is that, if you disregard to be gentle, you disregard your salvation.

And gentleness does not depend on quietness or self-respect but it depends on self-control and honesty. Why do you need to be gentle? And what is my main concern about gentleness?

The world we live in has different kinds of behaviour or conduct. There is nothing to be compared or explain be about our existence.

Everyone has his or her character which is different from another because of sin. There are differences in conducts and ability. But gentleness brings unity and equality among men.

We all need to be gentle if it is possible and to do away partiality. It is not your duty to show who is correct and who is not, but it is your duty to let others feel at home.

We all have what makes us and what each one can do and cannot do. Our basic duty is to help the weak and comfort them. Many people have failed because of a negative attitude towards each other.

My concern about this content is to let you know the beauty of been moderate and the fruit it can bear.

Do not overlook the laws of life and never disregard discipline, and do not be too known but learn to be gentle and then make the differences in life. Kindness welcomes people and makes them happy. It is a sister of joy and the brother of love.

If you want to live long and be at peace then you need to be kind or thoughtful. The most beautiful conduct or character is to be gentle or self-control.

Our health and wellness mostly depend on gentleness in all matters of life. Many fails of this character and others disregard gentility.

If you want to progress in life then regard gentility or self-control. Life cleanliness is the art of gentleness and the most beautiful character is self-control.

Sometimes others will say gentility cannot be useful in the mass congregation. But it is a big mistake to do away gentility in the crowd of people.

It is doom to act strange when you are in the stage performing amongst different people. Here, to go up or down will depend on your conduct reveal.

You cannot do away gentility in any stage of life, if you dare, you will disgrace yourself. Any type of appearance that considers not or lack gentility fails of integrity. And it is not good to be less in a gentle life.

Our ways and doings require tender to make things well. You need not go to school to pursue this kind of gift but it is a wish or will to obtain.

Why we all need to have this gift? (Gentleness) We live in a world that has so many characters, and without this gift, the people in the world will lose total fairness and order.

Do not disregard to be gentle but do all your best to obtain this gift. You need to ask yourself; do I have self-control or gentility conduct?

To be flourishing and be successful in life, you need to be honest. Here, gentility contains all these characters. Do not disregard to be gentle or self-discipline, else you will lose respect and welcome.

Try and do your best to obtain self-discipline and build your city with love and joy. You need to practice how to talk in a polite way to others and then gain your self-esteem from your listener.

Be gentle when you are eating; be gentle when you are talking and walking. You need to keep yourself well and then to bring what benefit others and promote life. Do not be too gentle or abuse your gentility but let it be without bad comments.

To be original not a copy is an art of decent demeanour and modest life. Life is not about bragging but it is of good use of time and quiet spirit. You cannot build your life with empty ingredients but with ingredients that have unique identities.

Many will be failing if they do away an honest ingredient that calls for a good name. You need to be honest; you need to be forceful and gentle.

The meek shall obtain the earth and those who love the purity of heart will see God. It is better to lose all the world belongings than to lose integrity.

Oh! My dear, why throwing your beauty on the ground and why are you seeking money than knowledge? Be gentle and seek understanding and the difference amongst the thousand. Be gentle but not boast and be original not a copy to fulfil your mission.

4. Be Productive

God created man to be industrious and to maintain his wellbeing. Without this, there will be no happiness in human's life. The whole nature is move by industry and happiness.

It is a grievous mistake to overlook industry activities. Human nature is grown or progress by activities and there is no growth or development without industries.

Our development; service and life reasons all depend on industrial activities. To be a man is to be industrious. In fact, our nature is set by activities and there is no other thing which can help a human being to advance without that.

The industry is a human life remedy that makes a man present and reasonable. The world is move by activities and industries. What do I mean to be industrious?

I want you to learn something with seriousness, and do not go without this knowledge I am about to let you know. The system of man and the life of a man are built by industry. It is appointed for a man to work and then to survive.

Everyone has his or her working tool purposely to build his or her life to the end. The tool is the talent or gifts by which makes the life dear. And there is no one who lacks this tool.

But some of us wants to do away they're giving gifts which can create precious jewels for others benefit. Other too does not value their gifts but want to make a profit from the foreign once which are not theirs.

Means they want to live or survive through somebody idea to make wealth. It is a mistake to live by somebody's idea or makes someone gift or skill earn you profit.

When we use our gifts and combine with the other ones the world will bright and do away poverty from our societies.

We all have the idea or gift that can produce the necessary thing for the masses. Yet the absence of yours will make us lose the complete life benefit. The world needs you and wants you to make their life complete.

Do not keep your gift for no use but let it out to make someone benefit from yours. The success of others also needs yours for completion.

What do I want you to know or keep in mind? In fact, do not let your life useless but let someone benefit from you.

Do something that will benefit others through your gift or skills. You need to do something for recognition by your gift.

Never fold your hands but work by your own ability and make a difference in the world. You should not depend on someone's gift to living your life. But use your gift and make a difference.

Be industrious means be productive or fruitful and to be useful by others. That is, make your life dear and meaningful through your skills and your act of kindness.

Do not be lazy but work diligently by your talents to fulfil your mission. Many people want to live as having nothing to do or want to disregard their talents. Others do not want to think or use their mind for any purpose. Some also live aimless life and have no object before them.

We all need to ask ourselves the reason why we are here on earth? It is not by accident to be on earth today. You have something to do for God and others.

Do not bury your talent by means of cherishing others gifts than your own. But make use of your own for your progress and other's needs.

Do you know your gift is the aid for someone? Have to ask yourself why you have that gift or that gift has been given to you?

The world development and the existence of a man depend on these talents given. Everyone on this earth will be going to account for the gift given by God.

Our gifts are machines for creativity and the remedy for a quality life. Without the use of these gifts, a man cannot survive. So, it is a sin to bury your gift for no use. To live is to work and to work is to live but without talent or skill, there will be no productivity.

So, life is about industry and activeness. Industry brings development and meaning of life. We need to be creative and active as well. Those who disregard industry disregard life continuity and wellbeing.

We were created to be creative and to serve through giving concerning what we have created through our gift. Everyone has a part to play and to serve through the performance of his or her skill.

Our gift varies from each other and they all have the purpose of serving. Some are musicians; accountants, drafters, teachers, engineers, doctors and so on. All these skills play a role in man development.

Be original not a copy as the title this book wants us to know the usage of every gift and importance of each gift or skill. I want you to know the purpose of your gift and how important it is.

Everyone has what makes his or her wealth and there is no one without talent for his or her journey. The reason why I am making these comments is that I want you to know that you are useful and someone needs you to be able to survive.

You should not depend only on others gift to live and leave yours as nothing. If you do that, you will not be successful in life until death. You need to use your gift and multiply it.

Until you haven't done this, your mission on this earth is not yet fulfilled. The industry is all about trade or businesses on this earth. But those who want to live a cheap life disregard industry.

The hardships and other abusive life depend on regardless of industry. Others become thieves and murderers due to lack of industry and regardless of talent usage.

In fact, the increase of poverty in our societies or the world today stands on talents that are not used or buried. You need to use your talent to reduce poverty in our societies.

Be industrious and make life profitable. Many people have buried their gift and want others to serve them than to serve others.

There are many gifts or talents that hold knowledge and success keys which can open doors of progress and then bring comfort to others, but they have been buried by the managers who own it. And yet these people are complaining and accusing those who are using their gift.

One thing that is annoyed is that, when these people see their brothers who have become rich through their talent activities, they envy them for being rich. Let consider what the bible is saying:

Proverbs 6:6-11.

Go to the ant, O sluggard;

consider her ways, and be wise. Without having any chief, officer, or ruler, she prepares her bread in summer and gathers her food in harvest. How long will you lie there, O sluggard? When will you arise from your sleep?

A little sleep, a little slumber, a little folding of the hands to rest, and poverty will come upon you like a robber and want like an armed man.

One thing we must all know is that those who are not willing to use their talents are lazy and timid. These people cannot inherit the new earth and they have no excuse concerning their gifts.

The today miserable states of some people are from misuse and unused talents given to them by God. We are created to be creative and responsible. We have no excuse of not using our gifts and cannot escape from doom.

We have part or role to play and it is our duty but not anyone else. Ones again let note this scripture:

Mathew 25: 14-30

"For it will be like a man going on a journey, who called his servants and entrusted to them his property. To one he gave five talents, to another two, to another one, to each according to his ability.

Then he went away. He who had received the five talents went at once and traded with them, and he made five talents more.

So also he who had the two talents made two talents more. But he who had received the one talent went and dug in the ground and hid his master's money.

Now after a long time, the master of those servants came and settled accounts with them. And he who had received the five talents came forward, bringing five talents more, saying,

'Master, you delivered to me five talents; here, I have made five talents more.' His master said to him, 'Well done, good and faithful servant.

You have been faithful over a little; I will set you over much. Enter into the joy of your master.' And he also who had the two talents came forward, saying, 'Master, you delivered to me two talents; here, I have made two talents more.' His master said to him, 'Well done, good and faithful servant. You have been faithful over a little; I will set you over much. Enter into the joy of your master.'

He also who had received the one talent came forward, saying, 'Master, I knew you to be a hard man, reaping where you did not sow, and gathering where you scattered no seed, so I was afraid, and I went and hid your talent in the ground.

Here, you have what is yours.' But his master answered him, 'You wicked and slothful servant! You knew that I reap where I have not sown and gather where I scattered no seed?

Then you ought to have invested my money with the bankers, and at my coming, I should have received what was my own with interest. So take the talent from him and give it to him who has the ten talents.

For everyone who has will more be given, and he will have an abundance. But from the one who has not, even what he has will be taken away. And cast the worthless servant into the outer darkness. In that place, there will be weeping and gnashing of teeth.'

We need to use our given gifts and to fulfil the Master's interest. So, when He comes then we will be able to account and welcome Him as well.

Everyone has what makes his or her life dear. There is no unskilled human being on earth and there is no one who can say; I do not have gift or talent. We need to be industrious and active. Life is about work and happiness.

It is our duty to change the world and make it comfortable by using our gifts for activities. There is no useless gift and an unskilled human being, every gift whether is one or two have what it can do and cannot be margin.

Naturally, everyone has a gift and ability to do his or her part as a human being. My concern is to let you know that you can do your best of your time and make a difference for the benefit of the world.

If we look at an ant and the termites they are weaker but they teach industry and activeness in life matters. How will you describe yourself? Who are you? And what is your duty?

In fact, there is no fire without smoke and there is no smoke without fire. What do I mean? If you regret to use your talent, you regret your progress and fame. And again you do away your name and your blessing.

Let no one think that, there is a way in which you can prosper than using your talent or gift. If daring, then you will be a thief in whatsoever you are doing, and it will not go well with you.

The industry makes life better and does away sickness; poverty and stress. It built the city and furbishes the old country. It progresses life and builds a sound mind and healthy body.

Be industrious and make a difference in life and glorify your Maker! Never ever put aside your ability and never wait for chance or opportunity before acting but do your best and let others benefit from it. You will be welcome by great men.

Be diligent and keep learning new things to better your grade. Do not throw away your dignity but maintain it and then receive great reward through your activeness and faithfulness.

Be productive and help others to be enjoying with you. Let others bless you concerning your industry and good works. As a matured man, you should not depend on others for food but do your best and something by your gift for your development.

5. Keep your words

Let your word be sure or certain. Never deceive through your sayings but be faithful in whatever you are doing and saying. Do not be as weather which changes but let your words has a position.

Means say the truth but do not mix your words with lies and truth. Keep your words but do not reveal the secrets of others. Let your words be yes, or no. Do not speak beyond the limit but to the limit to prevent lies.

Do not brag for profit but let your words mix with salt for good taste. Do not promise what you cannot fulfil but what you can accomplish.

Let words go with your act and do what you have said. Do not live a life contrary to your words but let words proof your dignity and be practical. Always say the truth and practice it. Be faithful in all your doings and keep on doing good.

Be aware of a man when speaking to him or mind your words before man. Do not pretend to say lies but tell the truth as due and keep on doing that.

As human beings, we always fall and do wrong but if we determine to do well, God accepts our thought and give us strength on that. The world is running out and there is no time to joke with.

We all need to be watchful and keep our steps well. There are a lot of lessons around us and that lessons are our guides making us know what to do next.

One thing we need to keep in mind is that there are enemies always want our fall and destruction. We should not make an attempt or think of wrongdoing, else we will be as nothing.

We need to keep ourselves well to prevent distrust. It is not good to pretend to be good but it is good to keep your words and practice them.

Manage to do good even to your enemies and never try to revenge when they wrong you. There are happens and misunderstandings between men; wars happing each day and night.

Who knows the result of each fight? Who will win the fight at the end? Who can identify the one among thousands? It is the only faith that can identify a man. What do I want to say or mean?

There is a unique thing in life and that is, saying and doing what you have proposed or doing what you have been said to do and again doing what you suppose to do.

This makes one's life unique and gentle. We need to keep our words and to prevent distrust. Who knows the mighty amongst the mightiest?

The one who keeps the words as from his or her mouth. The one who obey the laws and regulations and be able to complete the given assignment. Let your words be sweet and encouraging. Put away useless talk and let your words give life to your listener.

Do not rush when you are speaking but let your words flow a little slower to let your audience understand you better. Do not hesitate too long in your speech but make it timely as required for better understanding.

Never shout in your speech and again never be too slower in your speech to make your words boring and discouraging. Be neutral in your speech and make words cheerful and useful. Let's consider this scripture:

Matthew 12:35-37

The good person out of his good treasure brings forth good, and the evil person out of his evil treasure brings forth evil.

I tell you, on the day of judgment people will give account for every careless word they speak, for by your words you will be justified, and by your words, you will be condemned."

We will be going to account for every proceeded from the mouth. There is nothing that kills than the bad speech.

We need to well aware of every speech giving or voice out. We should not take words for granted but we need to mind every word proceeded from the mouth. Again let's note this scripture:

Ephesians 4:29 says;

Let no corrupting talk come out of your mouths, but only such as is good for building up, as fits the occasion, that it may give grace to those who hear.

It is our duty to make our words meaningful and beneficial to our listeners. We should not deceive ourselves in words and actions but we must be considerate about every speech proceeded from the mouth.

Many people joke about words and never mind the outcome. It is better to shout your mouth than to speak evil words.

We should not allow anger to control us and voice out badly. But we need to control every talk even when we are provoked by someone act.

We have an account to count and reward concerning it. We need to be vigil and keep our word well. It is late to say I am sorry but what can we do concerning the wrong words already proceeded from the mouth. We need to keep our words and make it reasonable to those around us.

6. Be Sensible

Moderation makes things right and beautiful. It is a food for the soul and life to the body and the spirit. Life is not about wealth and enjoyment but it is moderation in all doings.

Men cannot be totally satisfied without self-control and it is wrong to do away moderation in all matters of life. Do not avoid self-control in whatever you are doing. That is moderation.

The peak and the ideal life remained in moderate. You need to understand that, a good life does not depend on belongings or money. But it depends on a quiet spirit and in moderation. Sensitivity is the key of precious life that determined the result of anything we are doing.

The good life does not depend on been pompous or much wealth, but moderation in all stages of life. We are created to do things according to how it has been programmed, but not how we want it.

The good life does not depend on an abundance of wealth, but it depends on how you can cope with the little as well as the big in all condition without stress. We are to be careful in whatever we are doing.

We need not do things that are on call for but we must be considerate in all things. You should not fill water to the level or the edge of a pot or bucket, but with a certain level, else it will be difficult for you to carry or handle it.

What do I mean? Means you must be modest in all things to prevent trouble. Modesty in life brings peace, comfort and saves the soul from damage.

We need not force ourselves to be rich in a moment but we must gather it little by little for our own peace. Do not disregard moderation but make it your banner or logo in your everyday movement.

Do not dress in a manner that will draw attention but be moderate in your dressing. Do not eat more than the required amount but to the demand to prevent abuse.

Our diseases; discomforts, and others depending on regardless of moderation. We must do all things through modesty to prevent harm to ourselves. Even too much talk can damage your voice and your tone for the conversation.

It is not good to study or research more than the due time or above your strength. If you dare, you will damage your system and die unexpectedly.

We must be careful in all things and do thing according to our strength or ability. We must not stress ourselves for money-making out of rest but we must make money with mind and with care.

Your life must suit the time but not above or below of the time. That is, be moderate without question. Sometimes, we do things as of no mind and abuse ourselves as human beings.

We must not live a life as without law establishment but we need to consider all our doings and do things right. You cannot change your shape and neither can you modify your natural beauty, unless you abuse it or destroy yourself.

So, why are you forcing yourself on what you cannot get? Be vigilant and do things right for your own good and make your life dear.

Never makes-up like a polish shoe but be natural and maintain your beauty. Be not be too natural either be neutral but prove your identity with modest without comments.

It is not good to be too simple and neither to be too high but state yourself as water with no stain which is good to drink.

That is, appear with no remarks but as of good comments. Modesty makes life cherished or dear. Do not dress for attraction but dress to prevent nakedness and shamefulness.

The only key that opens the hardest lock is humility. Modesty is the art of meekness or gentility. Everyone in the world must keep in mind that, you cannot inherit the new earth without meekness or modest character.

We all need to know that modesty surpasses money and wealth. Yet there is nothing you compare in terms of attitude and behaviour.

It opens ways for improvement and prosperity. It is a big mistake to live without modesty and it will hard to succeed without moderation. In all human activities, modesty is a tool that builds good health and makes things well balanced.

One thing we need is modest and that without modesty, this world cannot be well managed. It is our duty and right to live in moderation.

Be original not a copy as this book title makes us know the importance of originality and the uniqueness of life without likeness.

God loves a modest life and wish to make that life dear and glorify. So, if you avoid a modest life, you avoid the beauty of character and the real motive of life.

My idea is to let you know that, you cannot fulfil your originality without these fruits. And where can you find these characters? Unless you allow Christ or The Holy Spirit to sit in you! Else, you will be out from all these seeds and your life cannot be accepted by God at the end of this world. Be moderate and keep on in moderation.

7. Sustain your dignity

Why are you throwing out your respect because of money? And again why you are putting away your beauty because of food? Never disgrace yourself for money and food sake.

A good life is not built by food and money, but it is built through self-respect and God-fearing. Do not lose respect before children and never be of any use because of your deceptions.

Many people have thrown their dignity because of their stomach or what they will eat and cloth. We need to keep ourselves from corruption or bribery. Many people have lost their dignity because of food.

It is a disgrace to fight on food. It is not easy to maintain your dignity if look at how the world is moving and the hardships that are pressing man in today's world.

But you need to maintain it in all conditions. If you look at the condition we are in today, it's always pushing you to think of what you suppose not to do or what against God's Law.

Others fail to keep themselves from wrongdoing because of the pressure. My advice to you is to wait for God's time and keep yourself from wrongdoing.

Never let someone to entice you and to do what you are not supposed to do. Always know your right but do the right thing for the sake of God's name. (Hallow be His Name) Life is not fair and it is hard to maintain your faithfulness.

Do not let your mind be crowded by the world beauty and its entertainments but build your hope in God and put your trust in Him.

Do not give up because of the pressures of the world. Who knows the evil hour or the day of reckoning concerning our deeds? Do you know the day that death will visit you?

Have you thought of the results or the reward you will get? Sometimes, your mind will tell you everything is okay, do what you like and enjoy yourself all is right.

My brother or sister, you cannot live a twofold life when it comes to salvation. That is, you cannot accept evil and good to live in one room and think that it's okay.

Your life cannot be accepted by God when you live such a life and there is no way to please God by accepting little sin to live in your room. You need to show your stand because the way to heaven is one and there is one wish that needs acceptance.

Here, you cannot be accepted, if you wish to live with evil deeds. Do not put away your dignity and never disgrace yourself by lying.

You must show your stand and prove beyond doubt or distrust through self-respect that you are a child of God. And there is no way for evil deeds. Else, you will lose your dignity as a Heaven child.

Be alert, to tell the truth, and act kindly for the glory of God. This is not done by might but by His Spirit. To them, that believe Him, and the many that believe in His Name gave them the power to become the sons of God.

This means that they put God first in all their doings and honour His Name in all their life. Sometimes you be discouraged by circumstances but you should not let put your confidence out.

Always remember that God is with you and He will help you to achieve your goal in life. In fact, there are a lot of circumstances that are disturbing our peace always. But should not forget that God has promised us and He will keep his promise.

He will not forsake or abandoned us. We need not fear or trouble hearted. But we need to have hope and remember that he is always with us to assist. We should not fear for want and be trouble hearted for the sake of what we will eat or cloth. Let's consider these scriptures:

Matthew 6:30-33 and John 14:1, 2.

But if God so clothes the grass of the field, which today is alive and tomorrow is thrown into the oven, will he not much more clothe you, O you of little faith? Therefore do not be anxious, saying, 'What shall we eat?' or 'What shall we drink?' or 'What shall we wear?' For the Gentiles seek after all these things, and your heavenly Father knows that you need them all.

But seek first the kingdom of God and his righteousness, and all these things will be added to you. "Let not your hearts be troubled. Believe in God; believe also in me.

In my Father's house are many rooms. If it were not so, would I have told you that I go to prepare a place for you?

If we consider these scriptures, it tells us that, we shouldn't worry about this life concerning life matters, but we should have hope in God and trust Him concerning what He has promised us.

So, there is no need for us to deceive for food or put away our dignity for want of money. But we must face life in all circumstances with truthfulness and allegiance to God. Let us note that, whatever act we intend to do, we will account for it. There is no need for us to act contrary to the sake of money or throw away our self-esteem for food or any kind of life lack. You need to maintain your dignity and glorify God by your doing and then put away indecent act.

8. Be Persistent

Life is all about endurance and waiting. The penalties of life are caused by a lack of patience. Many have failed in life because of a lack of patience and waiting.

Patient consists of meekness; forbearing and perseverance. It has the art of forgiveness and knows how to deal with everyone. Patience is the art of love and peace. Its build unity and calls for improvement.

Correct and beauty of life is built by forbearance without this, we can't achieve the quality of life. It is the art of self-control and the result of love.

In fact, we cannot live without persistence and cannot properly develop without persevering. We can only build the bridge across the ocean through forbearance and persistent. That is, life cannot be built without patience and carefulness.

Our life needs a wholesome ingredient to be able to achieve its goal. Life is about proper management and how we want it to be, but without patient, there will be no improvement.

Be patient in whatever you are doing and never be stressful in doing your work or everything you are doing. In fact, patience makes things well and best than what you can imagine. Without patience, there can be no life or living.

If you want to be a great man or woman in the world and the world to come, you need to be patient. You cannot do anything well without patient and cannot be a hero without endurance.

Best life and well balance life is built through the struggle with patience or fortitude. God always train us through circumstances to let us have the gift of a patient. Without that, we can lose our life and the aim by which He intended or planned.

He (God) always makes us walk through fires and rivers in life to have the gift of patience. Everyone who wants to have things on the silver platter fails in life and lost the beauty of life and its benefits.

We all need the spirit of endurance to have the peak of life. You need to be patient when you are eating and need to be patient when you are drinking.

You need to be patient when you are working and be patient when you are not working. You need to have patience when you are reading to get a better understanding of what you are reading.

Why you need patient in whatever you are doing? Patience goes with time and time goes with patience, if you do away patience, you do away time and life!

Our system needs comfort, peace and better understanding to achieve life goals, and this stands on the spirit of patience before all these can be achieved.

The best massive success and revenge of life is to be patient through hardship to earn your goal at the end. You cannot survive without patient and cannot work correctly without longsuffering. The one who lacks patient destroys everything that makes life good.

Never abuse yourself for quick money but be patient and acquire skills to make money. Do not seek for short way to earn money but set up your business to earn profits and comfort earnings.

You cannot do this without patience and focus. In fact, to make it best and beautiful in the life you need to have serenity.

There is no way for better and peaceful life without fortitude or courage. To make it well and sound it needs patience and continues the practice.

There can be no victory without patience and there can be no achievement without fortitude. Many people of today forget to have a good life and good living because of impatience.

Others built their life on someone knowledge instead of their own knowledge. Many others have lost their goals for the lack of patience. Many others do not have the spirit of waiting and forbearance.

Life is about patience and management in all conditions. It is not good to rush in life but it is good to have patience in all your doings.

There is no victory without war and there is no good result without patience.

In fact, patience makes everything that we do prosper and balanced. We all need forbearance to make life best and beautiful.

It is better to walk than to run on the asphalt road and it is better to be late in life than to be first in life and without the precious reward.

This means that you should not rush in whatever you are doing but be patient and move with the time but not above the time.

Patience built the lost identity and magnifies the poorest among men. Means the one who has patience makes a good name through that and become well known in society. Why don't you have fortitude and gain the most of life and be at peace? You cannot be able to do a thing well without forbearance and understanding.

Everyone who has patience has understanding and discernment heart. In fact, in order to prevent conflict from marriages and other institution, it stands on patience and understanding.

The absences of this fruit (patience) can cause a lot of misunderstanding and end in combat. The world development and peace stand on endurance and understanding.

Any country in the world cannot properly advance when there is a misunderstanding between the people, and this is caused by a lack of patience and understanding.

We all need the patience to develop well and to make things achievable. The Africans lack this fruit that is why they lack development or still standing today for no good achievement.

You need to put aside the haughty spirit and build your life with patience. Try to do things with patience and make it well and best. Be patience in your studies and other research works, for proper understanding to avoid mistakes and false theory. Whatever we are doing needs patients to come out with the best results.

Our victory; our progress and all that concerns life victory and proper development stands on patients to gain all the benefit of life. You can even count the sand of the sea if you have patience.

I mean you can achieve the best for life by patience and humility. Today many people want the best and beautiful lifestyle but fail of forbearance. Others demand through arrogance and force for life beauty, but what will be the result if it is out of serenity?

In fact, all the hardships that we are going through are testing our endurance for victory and not what we can gain without life.

So, patience is needed in all the stages of life for victory and best reward. We must put aside rushing for world goods and then build a life through serenity and humility. If you want to live long and have good health and better prosperity, then have patience and be at peace.

Our sickness and other grievous disease are caused by impatience. If you want to be a good manager and build the best relationship with others to preserve your name; then patience is your book for best records.

9. Keep your time

Time is life and everything concerning living through a period that is due. The world was created sequentially by God.

All that we can do depend on time and the ability to do stand on time. As human beings, our time today is short through sin and its existence.

The meaningful life and the benefits of life depend on time. The stages of life or time give us lessons to study each day and night.

We need not joke of time but we must make use of it. In fact, if we fail to keep our time, we fail to have life and the best of life and if we joke of time, we joke of eternity.

What can we do if we have time or not? What will be our reward, if we keep our time? In fact, many people have lost the precious things due to the waste of precious time.

Others too have missed their purpose in life due to the waste of time. Many others have missed their beautiful wives and husbands through the failure of time management. Some are over age but now searching for work at their old age; of which their bodies are weak to do.

If you do not use your time well today, you will walk without shoe at your old age. What do I mean? Means you will find it difficult to survive and lose hope.

You will lose happiness and life reward. Our life is built on time and the use of time. The success of life does not depend on how fast you can move but it depends on good management of time and the ability to making use of it.

Anyone who disregards time, disregard the glory and beauty of life. Everyone who wastes time for no improves becomes the enemy of God. That person makes God afraid or sorry for made him or her.

You need not waste time and do not waste a second for no improvement. You need to stop unnecessary conversation with others but let your conversation be profitable. The one who values time; values life and get the best reward from the time management.

Time helps us to make a good habit of organizing and structuring our daily activities. **Time** plays a significant role in our lives. If we better understand the **time** value, then it can gain experience and develop skills over **time**.

Time can also heal things whether external wounds or feelings and built the broken bones for hope. Here, if you have time and manage it well, you have everything.

Time makes hope and built the future. Time is precious and priceless for everyone, so we should not waste time.

We should use our time properly in a positive manner. Time is more than money and valuable than riches. You cannot compare anything time and time holds hope and courage. It builds

confidence and comfortability for the one who uses it well. You need to watch out and be careful of your time. Do not put aside timekeeping but avoid time-wasting. It is better to lose a gold than to lose a minute without profit. We make money through time and built a life by time.

Many have ruined their life due to time-wasting. Others have died without hope because of regardless of time. You need to keep your time for a correct account and to keep confidence.

You cannot redeem the time that is lost for no improve. But you can build the lost back by keeping rest of the time through hard work and enthusiasm.

It is better to be late to build the best life by time than to be first and waste the precious life for no moral improvement. Never waste a minute with no improvement but make use of each time for future harvest.

Our life bears fruit but a leaf. It must develop through time management and accomplish its goal. Time is a gift and it is important and precious than any gift that God has given to us. But many people fail to use the time properly.

It is a grave mistake to joke or misuse the time that we have as human beings. Time is all about life and everything done on earth. If you misuse time, you miss using eternity and every precious thing. You need to serious in life and be a timekeeper.

One thing we need to know is that life cannot be a life without time. So, life is time and time is life. Many people say time is money, but I say time cannot be money, but time is what you can make out from that period or the wise use of every moment makes wealth.

Be original not a copy as this book title, making us know the differences among men and the responsible ones and the beauty of their originality.

Upon the right improvement of our time depends on our success in acquiring knowledge and mental culture. It is our duty to develop the knowledge we have with the time.

To cultivate the intellect needed for work and to prevent poverty. To deal with the unfavourable surroundings which are not good for health, and let's make every moment a treasure and then mind every second for a good profit; We all need to build on time and not out of time and take time as unredeemable treasure and more than the precious.

God will bless those who respect the time and make use of it. It is your life and everything; so keep your time than anything that deserves to keep and then fulfil your mission.

10. Keep on doing

Our life is too short and with frustrations. It is difficult to live a good life when you look at the matters concerning it. But every faithful servant work towards his or her master's goal.

We have been given gifts for work and production. And you need to use that gift for profit. Everyone needs to work and be active for the best reward.

Our life has been subjected to work and production. And we all need to be busy for something and not to be busy for nothing. We must do away unnecessary conversation and work for a profit.

We must work as a sea for abundant profit and not for scarce. It is better to eat to a full and not for insufficient. Many people are busy for nothing and others are unproductive.

Many people do not want to work but to eat what others have work for. Such people are lazy and abhorring in society. Sea does not rest; it's always working day and night. What lesson it teaches us and what must we learn from its waves that always pending? What do I mean to work as a sea? As human beings, we have an assignment which needs a solution.

Our life has been programming or planned for a specific purpose or goal to reach and that is an eternity. Everything concerning eternity does not cease to work. And it always needs a production for other use.

That is how God created us to be. We are His likeness and image and we need to produce but not as unproductive. That is why we need to work and be fruitful and multiplying.

A sea wave teaches industry and production just as an ant. It's teaching us how to work diligently and actively in labor, and it's giving us note for everyday living.

We all need to work hard and build a life for eternity. Though death has taken in charge of our being to cease us from working continually, but we must work for life.

We should not be lazy but active in labor. Work keeps us fit and prevent poverty. It makes us productive and wellbeing.

It prevents us from growing old prematurely and makes us young at all time. We need to build a sound life and fit body through hard work. If you fail to work, you fail to live but if you wish to work, you wish to survive.

Life is work and work is time and life. If you joke of your work, you joke of your time and life. Work brings wealth and saves the needy. It is a barrier against poverty and loss of hope.

Its built confidence and courage. It does away fear and revives the soul. Building life without work is as planting the seed in the drying season or crossing the sea without a boat.

It will be difficult for you to make living without work. Your life will be nothing if you are not working. Work makes life and builds broken walls. Means it makes you feel better and fills <u>you with</u> joy.

Do not be sleepwalker but be ready to work and live well. It is not good to be idle but work with hands and make the difference in life for the glory of God.

In whatever we are doing must be done in the right way to prevent distrust and wellbeing. We all need to work prevent being a burden for others and our families. It is good to work and enjoy a good life and share responsibilities.

Do not joke when you are working and do not work to abuse your health. You must work according to your ability and do not look at a time when you are working.

You must be alert and do what you can. Do not misuse your time but make use of it and make profitable. Work according to time but do not measure the time with your work. That is work tirelessly but do not abuse yourself by overwork.

Be consistent in your work and work correctly but try to prevent idleness. It is your duty to make your work beautiful and interesting. You must take every work serious and lovable to prevent laziness.

So, work as a sea means to be consistent in your work and do not joke about it. Work and make work enjoyable. Do not be discouraged when things go wrong and do not dishearten when your work goes down.

In fact, I have been in stages that are difficult to explain. Hardship has taught me a lot of lessons and has opened my mind for better things.

Every good worker will meet disappointment and unbelievable things but do not be overwhelmed, continue just as the condition has led you into and try to prove your inner being.

In all be faithful in your work and do not be lazy in your work. Do not make work a burden for you but make work enjoyable and interesting.

May God keep you on track and do things better. Do not forget to work as a Sea. That is keeping your consistency in work and proves beyond doubt.

11. Think and Act

Do not close your eyes and do things as the mad man in life. The rivers have their channels and all other things have a lane for a living.

Do not go to the right or to the left without the correct reason. Never fight or talk with no reason. But know the time and hour that is reasonable.

Do things that favor's all those around you. Do not go beyond the line or do not cross the demarcation line. Know the difference between day and the night.

Do not worry when somebody hurt you. Be patient in your speech and know how to communicate with others.

Do not rush when doing something. Consider your speech at each hour and know the time to voice out. Eat sufficiently, do not over eat but measure what is before you, and then prevent greedily.

Do not mislead others with your false thought. Do not frame words that do not benefit. Cause no alarm without a thief; means never draw people's attention for no reason.

Manage your house, not the others and do not conclude your message without meaning. Always know the right time and the reasonable hour to say no or yes.

Make your speech simple and reasonable. Dress decent and wear decent shoes. Means do not be a stumbling block to others.

Do not say any word or add any word concerning what you have been sent to say. Do not hesitate to do well to others, or give to others what you have. Do not rush to answer a word; if you have been asked to explain something.

Let your no be no, and you're yes be yes. It is your duty to make the choice on two different things. Never let others decide for you or choose for you as a child. Manage to control yourself when someone causes you to anger.

Do not mutter with one of your workers before his or her colleagues; you need to consider the sun and the moon and the stars.

Means do not separate the best friend by your false conversation. Do not shows love to one of your workers than the other. Try to prevent hatred among your employees.

We will be judged by our act or doings. Do not exchange somebody's rights through a bribe, and never turn judgment because of money. Consider your walk; your speech and so on.

Do not pretend to cause harm to your brother or sister. It is better to lose your gold than to let someone fall by your conduct. Ask when you do not know and seek if it is needed, and nock when you come before at the door of someone's room.

Do not act as if you did not have a mind. Search and study the difference between gold and silver. Do not mix oil with water to prove your ability; else you will fail because of the differences. Means never force yourself to do things you don't have any knowledge concerning it; and then to disgrace yourself. Give the wholesome food to others. Means say the right words to others and let them recognize you.

Do not dance without a song or act like a mad man. For you do not know who is coming, or what will happen in the next hour. Seek knowledge and wisdom that will help to differentiate the right from wrong.

Do not build the lights around you, whiles you know you are in darkness. Means do not show off and let others admire you through deception.

But be simple and act decency, so that, you will get help when you need help. Do not be wise at your own estimation but be humble and be merciful, then receive mercy.

Do not work with any heart, else you will earn a bad result. We are in the world with confusion and the dangers, but we need to manage all the conditions with a good heart and with reasonable conduct. When your enemy falls, do not dance at his or her presence. But show sympathy and then prevent provocation. Do not consider the mocking bird to flee without punishment. That is, punish your child on the wrong act and discipline him or her to take the good path.

Do not support the wrong act but reproof and correct the wrong child. Let your child praise you at your old age.

Do not seek the result of a conversation which you are not part. Why are you stressing yourself on somebody's interest? Think of yourself and consider the result of your life.

Do not be above simplicity in life or how you should live, but consider the life and pick the sufficient which makes life better and desirable.

Do not sound your friend secret to others, but consider the outcome and prevent yourself from damage. Always assumed the result of your act and behave well.

Do not compare an animal with a man on bases of looking down at him. Means do not discourage your brother or sister concerning his or her deficiency. But think and act decently.

12. Don't Rush

Life is not a race and it is not like the sea that is always busy. But it needs patience and control.

The mountain has trees but how can we find out the depth of the soil on top. So is life, we cannot find out the result.

But we can determine the outcome through the act of today's movement. Why are you rushing? Why are you compare or thinking you are late? A tree is not climbed by running; so as to life.

You cannot rush or run to make things done at a moment. As a song is arranged before singing, so life needs arrangement before it can be managed well.

Do not think you are late and you need to do things fast to get a better life. Days and years are set before us by God and life must track the same.

You cannot do anything about it. As the world consists of darkness and light, so as life be. And you cannot wake up one day and have all your needs on the same day.

As the world wasn't created in one day; so as life needs to be built with that series. The life needs to go by order and it must be built through days and years.

Be persistent in whatever you are doing and take heart. Do not rush in speaking. Do not rush in eating; do not rush to answer a question and so on.

In fact, you cannot wash your hands with only soap without water. And again, you cannot go with a single leg and you cannot run with a single led.

It is impossible. You need to understand the series in life and how to cope with all situations. What do I mean?

Everyone needs wholesome characters for his or her life to earn profitable ends. If you rush, you will miss the needed amenities and cause an accident to your life. Means you will either die before your time or lost a meaningful life.

Do not jump or run in life and again do not mark the time. But consider the way and the manner you behave. You need to move like a clock move, but don't go before or after the clock. Means keep your time and make use of it.

As you cannot run on the muddy ground, so you cannot run in life. It is better to be late in life than to rush and fail in life. As it is not lawful to use your two hands to eat; therefore, it is not lawful to rush or run in life.

Do not be too aggressive about your life to make things well. That is, do not force yourself to become rich. But take time, and reason about the best way you can manage to the best of your wish.

Why die before your time? Do not rush, for you don't know what tomorrow holds for you. Be patient and keep on managing, then fulfill your goal and earn a good destiny.

13. Don't be Careless

You need to mind your business and value every little thing. Do not take things for granted. Be serious in life and determine a positive result. Pick the little that have less attention and prepare it with days. Open your eyes and search for the best.

Do not mind to dig deep but consider every stage. Set the target but do not put aside the necessary tools for the life through rushing. Set your goal right but manage the rest.

Do not combine sugar and honey at the same time, but use them one after the other. Prepare yourself at each time and welcome negative and positive.

Know the difference between day and night. Do not misuse the time but make a profit each second. Control yourself at every hour and manage. Do things right but consider the outcome.

Do not move without considering your steps or do not move without your eyes. Means take care and move. Arrange your kitchen and prepare your food. That is, be decent in all stages of life.

Do not use two knives at the same time. That is, do things one after the other. Do not combine dogs and cats in the same Apartment. That is, you cannot rear two different animals in one cage.

Do not play two songs at the same time. Means do not put yourself into trouble without preparation.

Plan and do things in order. Set the target but manage the target. That is, work towards your goal but do not put aside what benefit others and you.

Do not cut the guideline. Means do not overlook the laws and regulations. Do not talk when you are walking alone. That is, don't behave like a mad man. Cover your mouth when coughing. Means close your mouth when you are eating.

Do not combine salt and sugar at the same time. That is, do not combine lies with the truth. Do not leave a stranger alone in your room.

That is, do not trust the person you did not know well. Do not answer a word without understanding.

Do not combine oil and water as one substance. Do not use oil to wash your hand like water. That is, do not replace bad for good or do not do things contrary to the law and order.

Do not sit on somebody's chair without his or her consent. Means do not steal someone's property without his or her approval.

Do not mix two different oils for profit. Means do not cheat others for prosperities sake. Do not forsake your old house in which you grow. Means do not disrespect your Mother or Father at their old age.

Do not compare two different ropes as the same. Means do not compare two different powers as the same. Go forward do not look back. That is, don't give up or be discouraged.

You need to dress up but do not forget your shoe. That is, don't overdress but dress decently. Do not let your shoes make a noise when walking on the street. Means dress with no attention towards you or dress modestly with no comments.

Do not talk over time or more than the required hour. Means talk like a reasonable man but not as a fool. Do not cross a small river on foot when it is raining. Means do not consider a small thing as of no value when you haven't experienced before.

Do not value yourself than others because of your beauty or exalt yourself concerning what you have, for you do not know the difference between today and tomorrow. Means you do not know what will happen today or tomorrow, so don't laugh at your friend.

Consider the poor and regard the aged at your harvest time. Means give to others who need your help today, for you don't know what tomorrow holds. It is unnecessary to run in your bedroom or the living room. That is, it is not a good or wise thing to rush when you are eating. Consider the wind and create windows at your room to keep it from heat. Means welcome people whom you did not know and they will bless you.

Respect the platform on which you are standing and do not run on it but consider its height, and then it will keep you from falling. Means respect those under you but do not disregard them; for they will let you prosper, and without them: you cannot stand.

Do not go before your master, but follow your master and learn from him. Always ask, if you don't know and don't be too known to cause your life into ruin.

Always try to do the best thing but do not exalt yourself about the good work done. Try to do the best of your time, when you are on duty at your workplace.

Do away laziness and be forceful. Consider every little thing, do not take it as light, else you will lose your dignity. Plan and do things in order. Never start your work without prayer. Be practical and manage any condition.

Do not be too high or do not be too simple, but be modest in the manner of no comments. Manage to welcome everyone and speak well or be attentive to anyone who you communicate with.

Be ready always and set your goals well, do not discourage by circumstance but go forward. Do not conclude your word without your viewers understanding, but make it clear to promote their peace.

Do not leave without concluding of your case, but settle it as it stands on you for peace. Know how to walk and talk in the house of God. Let your prayers be simple and reasonable.

Do not pray to please men, but pray from the heart and in humility. Stop conversation at the courtroom and consider your speech before the judge.

Respect and shut your mouth in the presence of the king. Do not be haste to answer a question but be considerate when answering.

Do not push yourself into trouble when there is no trouble. Means keep yourself at all times from the words of others.

Do not go before the thief or robber, else you will be adding by his or her punishment. Consider every act you proceed, and then have the good results. Do not say yes when the word is not true.

Do not shout when you are speaking to anybody. But consider your speech carefully in front of the rulers.

Do not cry at the wedding premises even when you do not agree. But control yourself till the end. That is, be wise and do the right thing in the presence of the mass congregation.

Do not joke before a lion, whiles you don't have a leg to run. That is, do not annoy the king in his palace with a false act without redeemer or the advocate.

Do not put your leg on somebody's shoulder and laugh at the same time. Means do not cheat your brother and convince him with your false words of comfort.

Do not mix salt and sugar in your mouth. That is, makes your words or speech clear for everyone to hear you well. Or do not deceive others by your words.

14. Understanding the Life

God created the world in days and through this process makes the life whole. In fact, the world has a lot of histories and messages that need attention.

As human beings, we need to consider everything that goes on every day. Humans' lives have a lot of lessons and the subjects that need to be studied.

Things that happen every day are calling us out to be watchful. We have so many incidents which serve as security.

Life cannot be straight or smooth every day. What we need to know is to manage and consider every situation. Things of this world have no peace and proper standing.

Many people have failed because of impatient and have damaged their life because of the lack of waiting. We must understand life and how it must be controlled. In this world, nothing comes by accident, but it is for our lessons and promotions or failures.

Life is subjected to failures and dangers, but all these are there for our progress. We must keep in mind that, we cannot enjoy good continuously, but sudden risk and others are part of our progress.

We should not make a noise when something bad happens to us. But we should know is part of life. There are many sounds of cry every day, and there is a joy as well. This life is mixed with good and bad because of our first parent sin.

The world has been damaged by sin. So things are not accurate as it was from the beginning. This has made life too hard for us as human beings.

We have the keys which can open every good thing that makes life better. But there is attack everywhere on the globe, which always resists us from reaching the best standard. And because of these attacks, you need to determine and have faith in God.

It is tough to manage life; if you are not determined. You can give up and do whatever you wish but later destroy your life forever.

Too much poverty can destroy your ability and can even shut you till the grave. Try and do something that will set your life at liberty and peace; and then continuing in searching for the best that makes others get benefit from you.

Do not fill up your cap only but fill others cap too. Means do not be selfish but support others of their needs.

You must understand that this world is not for the one man but for everyone born in it. That is, try to share with others what you have and enjoy with them and weep with them.

Do not cover your belonging for your own benefits; but let others use as their own property, that makes your blessings complete and enjoyable. You cannot complete your life without support from others. So, let others complete theirs with your support.

Do not be hard, but be flexible but not weak. Be humble but not dangerous. Be smart but not as the thief. Do not deceive by your appearance but do what people will admire you.

Try to live peacefully with your enemies but don't hate them; do them good and let them know you love them. It is difficult to love your enemy but that makes you unique.

Try and understand all these conditions, and then you will be fruitful. A good life is not like a running river which everyone can fetch and drink.

But it is like facing the desert wind blowing with dust. But requires forcefulness; perseverance, willingness and focused in order to pass through.

Those without these characters; will fail of a good life and its practice. Do not consider the sea wind or look to the waves but be focus and drive your boat to the shore.

So many people have failed because of cheap life and unfaithfulness. Those who want cheap life disregard the principles of a good life and how it must live. The good life has penalties and that penalties are the beacons of correct progress in life. You need to know the circumstances in life and how it must be managed.

Those who take note and keep in mind with correct heart makes the difference. But those who disregard and take the life as anything, abuse themselves.

Do your best and record the songs of life to better your life. Means take notes of every situation and set your life with the correct goal, and then harvest the peak of life.

Life stands on the way you want it. Everyone must know the reality of life and how we should live. As you cannot do away the footing of a building, so you cannot start life in the middle stage.

You need to start the life from scratch and end in the matured stage. That is, you must succeed in life whatever may be. Do not fill with sorrow when things become tough. But consider as a helping tool for your progress.

Master yourself through hardships and discover the best for your life. Do not be dismay or fear, but prove yourself as a workman who knows the best for the client.

Means makes your work as experience man whether you have experienced or not. So far as it is your fields do it excellently.

God will not try you according to what you cannot do, but on what you can do. Always try your best and do what you can, but don't be abused by the trial. You need to understand life in all matters of conditions but be serious at every stage.

Do not cry when you hurt by someone, it is part of life. Do not be annoyed by trials or angry on the basis of hardship you are going through. But be prudent and make it profitable.

15. Manage to Prevent Sorry

We always wrong in life every day but some pretend or intentionally wrong their friends and others. Some also consider wrong as nothing. But you cannot joke before a lion and take yourself free.

Do not consider an ant as of no value or feeble to do and then promote the elephant as the king of capable. Means do not look down on others who are less in stature and then admire the giant bodies. Do not consider giant bodies as those who can do as to the best.

Do not leave your master without seeking permission and later say I am sorry. Do not approach the king in his chamber without knocking. Consider the base of a building before starting the structure.

Do not wrong your master and leave him and later beg him for pardon. Be at peace with your master always and work from the heart. Be respectful and diligent in labor. Do not abuse your work mate with false accusations and later seek peace with him or her.

Consider every step you make and try to prevent regretful. Do your best to promote peace with all men and manage every condition. Do not leave the palace with running but consider your steps before the king.

Control your speech with time and prevent errors from your speech. Means know how to speak each time to others and then prevent sorry after the speech. Keep your time and prevent lateness at your workplace.

Do to others as you wish them to do for you. Be thankful and prevent greediness. Share equally to others who you work with when gifts are given to be shared with them.

Put outside envy in work when you are working with your colleagues. Do your best to encourage your associates in labor.

Do not work to please men but be faithful in your work and harvest the best result. Again never cheat in labor and later reveal your false labor.

Do not frame false news to distort the air but consider your speech and let the air blow at ease. Means do not confuse people by misleading them by your false message.

Always find out the truth and promote peace. Do not force yourself to be somebody by your appearance or do not carry the title you have no idea. Never wear the shoe that is more than your size and to cause yourself trouble.

Mind your word and polish it from mistakes. When you borrow, fulfill the payment; do not close your eyes on it. Be faithful in your speech and do not lie for favor.

Set your apartment with good atmosphere and then welcome people with good attention. Means do not confuse people for your own curse by misleading them and to hurt yourself at the end.

Always set your head up and consider the little. That is, mind those around you and consider the child as well. Study to the best end and then do your research well, to prevent distrust.

Do not run on the rough road with all your strength, but manage with the walk to prevent hurt. That is, keep your eyes with all matters of situation to prevent damage to yourself and others.

Set your goal with the correct level to prevent stress. That is, do not attempt what is not your field to disgrace yourself. Always wash your hands in running water to prevent sickness.

Means do the right things and then get good results. Speak with a salt to prevent tasteless from your speech. Means avoid useless talk in your speech.

Do not throw stones at night to disturb your community without meaning. That is, do not make noise on reasonable hours at the night with sound sleep. Do not bath with your shoes at home. Means do not act as a thoughtless.

Always do things in the light to prevent damage. Means let others witness about your doings with good comments. Do not work with measuring the time or keep your mind on time. But avoid measuring the time and work tirelessly but do not abuse yourself with overwork.

Do not consider the work as of whether small or big but do what you can by the truth, and from the correct heart. Do not trust a man by his word but by his act.

Never turn around and say it is done, whiles you know nothing has been done. Means do not lie to others on the bases of protecting yourself. Do not forget your keys when leaving home. Means prepare your-self well at any time.

Welcome two people equally, do not show partiality by regarding the one than the other. Do the right thing. Do not deceive by your appearance or pretend as gold.

Avoid show without acts or comments. That is, do not appear as a wealthy man or woman without capital. Do not jump before your enemy but consider your step at his or her presence. That is, seek peace and always do right at the presence of your enemy. Do not accept the case with only one witness but consider two witnesses for the judgment.

Do not put aside the right judgment or twist the judgment on the bases of enticement. Consider every case well and conclude with the right judgment.

Do not put aside the witnesses of any case brought to you as a judge. Then and again consider every little word before the pronouncement of the judgment.

Everyone has only a chance about his or her life to live. So do not kill someone by your word or act about anything you undertake.

Do not throw out or disregard the leftover grains, for it is food for the birds of the air. That is, do not be selfish and keep all the food for yourself.

But share or give out to others who need your help. Do not put off the light of the house to cause somebody's fall or hurt. But put on the light to keep the house from the darkness. That is, keep on entertaining others on your good works or acts.

But do not prevent others by your bad acts or behavior. Do not lie to your husband or wife on the basis of your selfish interest. But consider and tell the truth and promoting continuous peace and love.

Do not go before or after your husband or wife, when you are going to the same place. But move with or go together to strengthen the continuous faithfulness and to prevent disunity.

That is, keep closer to yourselves for profound love. Prevent conversation without introducing the friend or mate to the husband or wife as you are going together. Dress together and move together; that is, do not cover up anything to the wife or the husband.

Pour out the honey from its cup and share together the sweets and rejoice together. Appreciate the doings and prevent discouragement. Continue the dance to the end of the song to keep happiness to the end.

Do not over dance to abuse the sweetness of the song, but keep it on the track to prevent an accident. Manage to prevent sorry and consider the move.

Do not praise one child among your children or before the other children. Always keep silence or stop your conversation when you heard the noise at your backyard. That is, do not continue your speech, when there is a misunderstanding between you and your spouse.

Be silent when there is a shout or misunderstanding, to keep your continuous peace. Manage the bottom and the top. That is, cope with all the conditions or the situations with the good heart and patience.

Do not go beyond miles but the end with your mile and then prevent disrespect. That is, obey the rules of nature.

Do not overflow in your speech as a madman but control your speech and make your words simple and understandable. Always tell the truth and prevent confusion. Based on the facts and defend your case.

Put off the clumpy act and respect the aged. Be happy and manage the little or the big. Be thankful to God and move with all your good works and acts.

16. Do the Right Thing

Do not close your eyes and walk, but open your eyes and see. Do the right thing. Do the right thing, do not say yes, whiles the answer is no. do not run before your parents but run after them.

Do the right thing. Many people want to fill up their rooms and leave the whole building. Means do not hoard up by selfishness but give to others as you can.

Do the right thing. Respect men and wish them well. Do the right thing. Dress well, when leaving from home. Arrange your bed before leaving. That is, do not close your eyes from your responsibilities.

Do the right thing. Do not sweep your room and leave your corridor unprepared. That is, complete your responsibilities each day.

Do not put the light under the table, but on the table. Means do not cover what benefit others but share with them. Do the right thing whiles you have life. Help the needy and rescue the perishing. Share the big and small at the hours of want. Go with charity and truth always, and then seek to help the weak.

Do the right thing! Do not look down on others because of your wealth. Do not eat to the bottom but leave the rest to the birds. That is, do not be selfish concerning what you have, but give to others who need your help.

Do not leave the old woman or man alone to struggle. Means do not close your eyes from the destitute or the weaker that need your donation. Do the right thing!

Do not take away the sightless stick to cause him or her fall. That is, do not cheat the stranger at your home about his or her needs. Do the right thing!

Do not pass through the window, whiles there is a door. Means do things according to the required measures. Do not sleep on the bed contrary to yours. Means do not take somebody's wife like yours.

Do not go and shout at the front of kings' palace out of consideration. That is, do not go beyond the demarcation or break the moral law. Always seek to prevent war in the presence of your enemy and love at all times.

Do the right thing! Keep on your donations and do not consider your giving by means of seeking the reward. Help the stranger but consider your room, that is, serve the stranger as well but be vigilant.

Do not leave your keys for the one you do not know. Keep your eye on the ground and consider every weed. That is, know how to deal with others for good but with the eyes open. Rejoice with those who are in good condition and at the same time mourn with those who are mourning.

Do not leave the food uncovered and do not give to the stranger the unwholesome food. Do not mislead the stranger by cheating. But honor the stranger with a good welcome.

Do not go before the stranger or after the stranger who did not know where to step his or her feet. Do the right thing! Set the time well to prevent lateness.

Do not delay the worker's payment to keep on their worries. But pay prompt their wages and to prevent curse.

Do not argue with your worker on his payment. Do not force your worker to work overtime but consider his strength and health.

Do not put your worker into trouble because of your wealth. Give a reasonable amount of payment to your worker to prevent murmuring against you.

Do not let your worker cry before to receiving his or her payment. Give and continue in giving, support and makes people laugh with a good heart.

Do not close your door and shout people's out from your presence. Means welcome people with a good heart and with love. Complete your work with the correct report and the best result.

Do not use your tools for making unnecessary things. But let your tools work excellently.

17. Burning the weeds

Do not support the growth of weeds in your field. Do your best to throw out the poisonous substance or burn out the weeds in your field. Do not support the wicked on his or her actions.

Throw out the crack bottle and fill the fresh one. That is, do not waste your time on the unnecessary things. But make use of the time on the things that benefit.

Every fresh thing needs fresh and every old thing needs old. As you cannot dress a child with the aged attire, so to the life we are living. You cannot take life contrary to its principles.

Whatever you are doing must be on its way. What do I mean or want to say concerning this content; burning the growing weeds? Every practice in this world forms the character and grows for harvest.

The life we are living needs carefulness every day and night. We need not rest or stop in the way for the needless things. We need not entertain any weeds to occupy our fields of productions. That is, do not allow anything to entice you from your improvement. That is, determine on the things that bring peace to the soul.

Do away covetousness; selfishness, fornication, greedy, malice and so on. These are the weeds that make life standstill and then destroy the idea of life and make things worse. You need to know the best for your life and the fruit you must bear.

Do not cover the bucket when it is raining. Be ready at all time and make use of every minute. Do not allow someone to use your cup for drinking.

That is, do not allow people to look down on you because of your act or do not devalue yourself because of your poverty. This world has so many influences and the things that can destroy the soul for eternity.

Every act forms character and decides the position of the actor or the actress. Do not joke or jump before the lion as your playmate. Do not consider the drop of water as small or disregard the little act or doings as nothing. Who knows the penalties of one sin committed?

Do not take things for granted, every little substance has the value and its performance. Do not allow or entertain the stranger food on your table. Do not look the wine or considers its smoothness, it bites like a scorpion.

Do not take note of a woman or thought of her beauty, it destroys the spiritual giant. In fact, all the things on this world or everything which is done on this earth have the effect or the affect at the end.

But the one who considers and manage according to the right channel find his or her-self secure. We shouldn't allow the matters of this world take us captive. We need to shun everything that entices us into trouble.

Do not love the world or the things in the world; the one who loves the world has no love for God. This world is passing away but one who considers God will live. So, do not allow weeds to take over your farm or field. But clear the field with all the needed tools and then find rest and peace for your soul.

The world is going to an end but what will be your lot? How have you considered your act and doings? Every plant that does not produce good fruit will be root out.

Do not nurse the fruitless plant on your field or allow the growth of weeds. But do your best to care for the field, and everything on it. And then burn the unwanted materials from it. What do I want you to know?

Do not joke or allow things to take you captive. Take your life seriously and do things right and then fulfill your mission on this earth.

Do not dismantle your treasure or destroy your gold. But make things well and protect your soul from eternal doom.

Do not fill the broken bottles but fill the fresh bottles and then avoid waste. That is, do not waste your time on the needless things but on the necessary ones.

Do not wash the pig in the early morning but wash it at the night and protect your cloth. Consider your doing and prevent yourself from damage.

Do not water the unplanted field for the sake of preventing dust. That is, do not give to one who needs nothing or avoids giving to the rich and then prevents the curse to the entire family.

But refresh others by giving to the poor and then refresh yourself. Burn the growing weeds and then secures your place. Continuing on your good works but consider and avoid doing the things that are unprofitable.

Do not entertain evil at your doorstep to allow it into your room. Be vigilant and do things according to its right channel. Burn the growing weeds from your field. That is, keep your heart than anything that needs to be preserved.

18. The Bondage Worker

Many people have become slaves due to the choice of work. Their state as beings has no freedom and their skills are controlled by the other.

Many people have wasted their time, and have gained nothing because of the work chose. In fact, many noblemen have become slaves through their work.

There are many people who are working as slaves but have the ability to work on their own or create a job for others to do.

Many people have skills to create jobs but they are civil servants caring for the government jobs and controlled by the instruction to do their part as government workers. Others have been separated from their families and have no rest to even visit their loved ones.

In fact, doing work as a civil servant for the nation is not the problem, but to set your time management well makes you the slave. Why because you cannot manage to the best of your time as you wish. The worse thing is that the time you will realize, and then you are old to do the best of your wish for the family is over.

Many people have gone to school without the correct purpose and have wasted their precious time for nothing.

The Africans lack of creativity has led many of them to live a cheap life and has resulted in nothing. Today, many Africans are jobless because of their attitude and self-distrust that many of them never aim at.

They all want the government to do for them, and the very annoying thing is that; those who are scholars among them want the government to employ them and to appoint them in ministerial positions.

This is totally shaming; they can start from nothing to something that is to do for themselves and others who cannot do because of their mark or situation; that is lacking to do on bases of lack of skills. But these so-called academics looking to the government for their food as even handless, sorry, to hear this! But it is a fact.

Everyone must teach himself or herself before teaching someone else. We all need to serve, but we must create to serve, that is how God created us to serve.

You cannot serve without haven't something, and you cannot serve properly out of creativity, so you must create to serve and make the serving whole.

Our life must serve a good example to others as individuals and our actions must benefit others to promote the entire community. One thing that makes us slave is the way we want ourselves in this life and it is a choice.

Everyone has the ability to do for him or herself or create for the masses, but some have chosen in the way they think as best and easy to get wealth faster, but it has results their bondage. In this way, what am I wanted to suggest?

Many people have the ability or the skill to create the needed thing in life, but they have valueless their gift or the talent and want cheap money to live their life.

This has caused their slavery. The world we live in has what it takes to have the freedom of life concerning on our act and choice, but those who want cheap labor in other way have become slaves.

The one who wants to escape the middle age lost the experience and ends in hopeless. That is, others do not want to work and have the experience than to earn their wage but jump for quick money.

Never think you can have the sufficient for your life by working for somebody unless you steal or caused yourself ruin by working overtime; even you can end your life without achieving your goal.

I am here to let you know that, cheap living is cheap slavery and willing to work for someone is willing to be a slave, and willing to be a slave is willing to be hopeless for your future generation.

The workers of government institutions must note this. To serve your country is not bad at all, but to be a slave in your country on bases of what you will eat makes your slavery peak.

You cannot be a freedom worker whiles depends on someone's instruction to make move. And again you cannot manage your time as you wish whiles you can be posted to anywhere depend on somebody's command.

There is no freedom for the one who depends on command to move and to control their time by someone wish.

In life, you can choose to be a slave and make somebody controls your time for you and it is your choice to be a slave or not a slave to someone. The lives we have been subjected to two options either free or bond.

Our gift or talents are independent and it is up to the point as measured by God. That is able whether small or big, but you can allow somebody to control it for you by choice. And this suggests that you cannot use yours unless it is in subjection or control by someone.

Many people want to live a cheap life but end in slavery. There are people who have completed universities and colleges but want the government to find a job for them or employ them. This is very serious and embarrassing to those who want to depend on the government and to be able to survive.

In fact, those who want to live such a life are still babies, no matter their age or academics; I must say they are immature to do for themselves. If you are not agreeing, it is your notes to revise and rethink again about your condition as a human being.

Your life must have a goal and be able to decide for yourself and not to depend on somebody's decision to live your life. You can start something with the skills you have to acquire and find out where to start and what it must involve beginning something for your life and others.

If you cannot decide for yourself then, you will be a slave till death. As a mature human being, you should not let others teach you what to do unless you do not know, right? But you must be able to do for yourself and others too.

The knowledge we have must be in collective knowledge to serve us the best for the living and to bring us to the required at the end. That is why God gave each one the gift to serve the purpose to have the needful in the life for everyone.

The life development in general or as a country or in a community depends on the combination of skills put together in the manner of supporting each individual to have the required amount for the living.

We all need to serve by way of supporting each and every one by means of the knowledge we have, but not in subjection by someone's command in order to move.

Else the skill is not complete by its nature or chooses to be a slave. Many people are in ruins through their mindset and many of them are salves because of choice.

My concern is to let you know that, you can do the best of your time by means of setting up your own business through the little skill you have if you aim at.

Never let someone teach you what to do, while you know the best to do. And never be a slave, if you know what to do to survive. Build on your foundation and never lose hope, fill your holes and cast your floor and start to build your structure.

Let others know your ability and teach them by your action. Don't be a slave because of food, but prove yourself as a workman with all the skills in place.

Set up business, serve your country, love men, and women around you, keep the little as well as the big, keep the truth, manage the little and be vigilant when you fill up, live peace with all men and fear God!

19. The liberty Worker

There is a word that makes a man whole and there is work that set the life at liberty. Any human being has the ability to do and the will to choose the way that seems right to him or her. But the end makes the difference of the choice.

Liberty makes man the ability to possess and live to the expected end. Your will can make you a slave but the right choice can set you free. What is your aim concerning your life? And what are you heading towards? What do you want to be? How serious are you?

Many people are slaves because of what they will eat. Others are crying because of the work chose. Your ability makes you a man or woman and your aim set the position for you. Again your work defines your glory and set your wealth.

Everyone in this world has what it takes to manage the life and live to the best of a wish. But you can be nothing if you wish and you can be somebody if you will. So as to the work, we are doing. The work that we are doing makes our life and brings joy into our life. If you are jobless, means you are lifeless. Your job is your being and your being is a job. In fact, life without a job is vacuum or lifeless.

But the job that makes you a slave is hopeless and fruitless. The one who has the ability to the work but is subjected to an instruction to act or do lacks knowledge and understanding. Our abilities make us whole and value.

Who is the liberty worker and what benefit can he or she gain? In life, there are many ways and means that make the life better and peaceful.

But so many people want to achieve what they are not deserved. Others want a shortcut to earn the best and many others also want cheap the time and hoard up.

All these things make life stressful and meaningless. But the one who goes on time and manage to do the right thing set up the free life or makes the life beautiful for him or her. Everyone who wants the best for his or her life must acquire skillful knowledge and understanding to live.

The liberty worker is the one who uses his or her ability do for him or herself and for the others of the best without someone's instruction.

Everyone has the ability to set up a job and manage it. That is why God gave us skill according to our strength. And it is up to us to manage and improve it.

No one is out of means or without the seed to beginning something. But others plant theirs or hide their seed or talent on the salt sand and to make it fruitless.

Those are the ones who suffer want and become slaves at the same time. But ones, who use their talent and manage according to the time, set their life free and joy the best too. Do you want to be slave or royal?

Then set your mind well and plan the best for your future. Assess yourself and bring out something for your liberty. Else, you will be a slave in another persons' home. In order to have the best and be at liberty, you need to work for you own or set up business and manage it.

Never enslave yourself for quick money, but be patient and start your business on the bases of your strength and manage it according to the time.

Then free yourself from the bondage of government work and be the man of value or the woman with abilities. Let your skills set you free and be your own boss.

20. What is your interest?

What makes you happy? What do you wish to do every day? What do you crave for? Your way of life is your way of doing. Your way of doing is a way of your interest.

Interest is a wish or desire of things that makes you happy. It is a habit by which earns you something. So, your interest becomes your daily practice. Whatever you do defines your interest and keeps you going.

Anything that you patronize often or regularly becomes your interest. What do I want you to learn from this heading? You always make future through your daily concern.

Your job becomes your interest and your life. There are many things leading us into destruction. We always pay attention to unnecessary things than necessary ones.

These habits are leading us into ruin. You need to be careful in all your doings. It is important to keep note in all you're doings and come out with positive result. Do not take things for granted but take everything serious and keep watching. Having interest in anything leads to positive or negative result.

It is a passion of your being which you cannot live without it. So, it consists of art in creating of anything and sharing of things for the service of a man.

It is also consists of communication in any form of services to mankind. These are interest of people. Our services are the key element of our progresses in life. Many people are also mistaking through interest of the things they perform.

In all, what will your interest lead you to? The fact is that, those interests will show our stand and future improvement. You need to consider your way of lives and activities.

This forms our interest and habit that leads to the end. The future hope depends on today's interest and the habit we exhibited. The only way for true success of life is harvesting the good result of your interest and of your habit.

It is not what you will do that shows your fame. But it is what you will harvest at the end that determines the peak of habit and the interest you display today.

Your interest determine the amount of habit perform each day. But the habit makes the future glory or wreck. You need to mind your interest and then care your habit.

It is important to note every action proceed in each day life. Do not be careless in any move of your life; but consider every move and attempt you make in each move.

You always build your future in any act you exhibit and then show the kind of interest and habit you hold. You to need mind your interest and your habit, then consider your words and your actions.

Whatever you engage yourself in brings your ends. But the true and correct harvest comes by true commitment. Your interest builds your destiny but your habit determines the result. That is, what you will gain at the end.

My concern is to let you know the result of habit you form and the consequence of your interest. Do not entertain yourself in the thing that ends in vanity. Yet, entertain yourself in the things that bring hope and the future life.

Do not be lazy; be prudent and forceful in all matters of life. But mind your interest and habit which built your future and hope. What is your interest? What do you do?

Do not live as there is no end of life. But live as there is the end of life and judgment and then fulfill your mission and the good end in the coming age.

21. What are your daily events?

Interest leads to daily activities and the purpose of life. Your interest forms your purpose and then determines your ends. But the activities form the direction of life and the peak of future.

Do not be satisfy with your low standard; yet improve yourself through your daily activities for better recognition. Correct life is form through activeness and honesty.

Do not sit there or live without activity but be active and courageous. What are your daily activities? Where are you focusing? What type of work do you do? What is your purpose?

As tree grows by watering, so lives grow through activities. But the best of life comes by honest work and perseverance. So, your interest becomes your daily activities and life style. This form habit and then makes future.

Your work determines your income and wealth. So, your activities determine your stand tomorrow. Today's fruitless lives of some people are cause by inactivity and procrastination. Do not live without activity but consider also the kind of activities you engage yourself in. Consider your duties and your doings carefully.

Do not joke of any act you proceed, but be watchful and set your steps right. You need to attend to your duties on time in each day, but do not work to abuse the time with no fruit.

That is work honestly and forcefully. It is important to know the end of every activity or the habit you have form. There are a lot of activities out there resulting in life and death.

It is also important to plan and think of everything you engage yourself in. Do not take things for granted but take note of every step you make and then do things right. Let your words and actions prove your identity.

Do not valueless the little things, but be considerate in all things and then know how to step your foot. Do not misuse the time but make use of the time through your activities.

What is your main work? What do you engage yourself in? How have you benefit from those activities? Whatever you engage yourself makes your life and builds your future.

Do not let the world deceive you or control by the things in it. Also, let not your activities close your eyes from necessary things and then forget people who need your help and your maker.

Many people have surrounded themselves with many activities that lead to nothing. It is a sin to close your eyes from people who need your help through activities.

This habit can lead you to destruction without any warning or signal. So, you need to be considerate and keep certain things well. Stop busy for nothing and then pay attention for other things that will keep your life save.

Do not pretend like busy man and close your eyes from others, but share your time with all those who are around you and prevent yourself from wreck. It is important to take note of others and then help them as you can.

Do not let your events prevent you from helping the weak. You need to have time for the big as well as the small. Means have time for your family and the people of your community.

I mean consider other things but not the single thing. Be careful in all your doings and then prevent damage at the end. Do not form a habit that will not benefit you at the end through your activities.

Yet make the most of your time by doing things that will earn you a profit at the end. So that, you will not live like regretful at the end through your doings. It is important to do the work that will earn you hope than hopeless.

Do not burden yourself through your activities. Yet do things on time to prevent burden. Do not take the world into your bosom. Do not carry a weight at the midday to abuse yourself.

Means rest when you are tired and relax when you are loaded. Do not carry all the burdens at a time, but take it one by one and reduce stress. Do not occupy all the time with many activities. But do things on time and one after another.

Be a good manager and then arrange things in order. Do not occupy two days' work to be done on one day. But let the day's work suit the day and the energy. In all, plan and do things according to the time and then prevent waste and unfruitful time.

What are your daily activities mean? It means do things on the right time and the right way for future hope, but not like hopeless and busy for nothing.

22. Sensible but destitute

You can start something as you wish. Though, you do not have means to start with. You can serve someone who has begun something to earn some income to begin yours.

It will take years but do not mind for the sake of your establishment. It is painful to be in poverty. But it is good to experience it for future management. Its build your ability to face every season in life.

Do not give up and make it a help to you. You do not have but you have when you make it happen. That is, be practical and continue in faithfulness.

You can do but its needs means to start with. Where are you going to that means to start with? In fact, it is sad, when you want to start something that needs means and you do not have that means to start with.

It is a heart breaking and dreadful incident. The man is prudent but lacks funds support his life journey. Who can help my situation or support me to achieve my goal? These the questions that come to mind of the one who want start business and have no means to start with. It is not how you see it, but it depends on the step you may take.

Worrying cannot solve it and guessing cannot let you there unless you move. You wish to do but how will you do it? This is the oat of a poor man that pains heart, wishes to do but lacks means to start off.

Many people have ideas but lacks means to support it. This makes a person a peak poor man by means of lacking funds to start what benefit the entire world.

What have you ask yourself about this situation and what lesson have you got from it? It is good to be poor and then know how poverty to people who are poor.

There is nothing that does not have a purpose in life when it happens. Those who are prudent but poor by nature have special appointment signed by God to them.

You should not take things for granted when you go through hardship. What lesson can you take from it? You know yourself and know you can do beyond doubt.

But you do not have the means to start with. This has made your life difficult and you do not know what to do or where to go to find answer to this problem.

It depends on you only and it requires your movement to making comes truth. In fact, honest living requires struggling. Life itself is not easy; but those who are not fortunate can be successful through honesty and willing.

Again, those who are very poor will be possibly become rich, if they aim to be or act towards it. It does not matter how great your poverty is, if you wish to be rich; you will be by God grace.

If you do not want to move ahead, then you will be stand still and will be as nothing. Though, you are prudent but poor; but you need to do something for your good and others welfare.

In life, poverty does not just come to a person but it has a purpose and reason which benefit us to rise up from one step to another or help us to improve our lives in it better stage.

So, when you become poor through a certain incident; do not be surprise, it is for your good. This life is contrary to our expectation and life is not rosy but hard.

You cannot be poor until the end of your life. Unless you yourself want it; Life can be better by your wish and it can worse by your wish.

A prudent in life becomes hero in wealth. Those who aim high and work towards it gain their wish. But those who do not aim at all remain the same.

Do not let it go, but do something about it. It will change for the better. It is your doom to be poor, but it is for you success, else you will not work towards your goal.

Poverty opens eyes of the people who are poor. It becomes blessing to who are rich and give to the poor. Poverty serves two purposes; it builds ability and experience.

It makes people receive blessing when they give or through giving. Prudent but penniless as this content; giving us lessons about wellbeing in society and the confidence that some of us for their future improvement in today's trials or circumstances that they may going through without of want.

It is better to be truthful when things went wrong in life and suffer for truth than dishonesty. But it is a doom to seek better life through thief or easiest way.

Life is not build in cool weather through relaxation. But it is built in the hot weather through hardship for better improve and have peace of mind.

This means, it is better for you to be prudent by means of establishing your own business than to depend on someone to have your food.

You will not get it as you wish and you cannot be free totally by working for somebody to have a living. You need to suffer to have your own, than to depend on others to have some part.

Be forceful and build your boot and set yourself free than to build someone's boot and be a slave until. Keep in mind that you can do it, no matter how hard it is.

You can do it and do it better than someone. You need to make difference by your practicality and set yourself free from penniless.

The peak poor man is you who are struggling to survive through honesty. Your reward will be awesome. Keep on in good work and build for many through faithfulness. Do not rest until you see it been fulfilled.

It depends on you bend the grace of God to make it alive. To become billionaire then you need to start your own business and then expend it.

You can become billionaire by aiming and set your mind on it through daily activities towards your goal. You need cease your poverty by attitude towards your work.

For Good Living and Knowledge Gain!
B. B. S. LIFE BOOKS.
The Academics Brains and Recreation Logics Page

Also by Bernard Benson Sarfo

The Fact Among Facts (1st)
The Fact Among Facts

Standalone
The Youth Murderer
Be Original Not a Copy
The Christians Science or Scholarship
Precious than Paradise
Habit makes future
A shelter from storm and rain
The Science of Life
The Strongest Lion Knockback
The Perfect and Inspiring City
Above Hope, Faith and Love
The Hero's Brave Decisions
The Weakest Among Plants
The Hero's Brave Decisions
Doing Above The Ability
The Wisdom Beyond Power And Greatness
Heavier Than the Heavens
The Academics Brains and Recreation Logics

About the Author

Bernard Benson Sarfo is an acquainted architectural designer and a motivational speaker.He is a gifted teacher who continues to motivate and encourage many.

Read more at https://www.amazon.com//author/bbslifebooks.